A Fucking Coloring Book

A SWEAR WORD COLORING BOOK FOR ADULTS

Kristie Color

Resting Bitch Face

The Forest Of Zero Fucks Given

www.ingramcontent.com/pod-product-compliance
Lightning Source LLC
Chambersburg PA
CBHW062201220526
45470CB00009B/2893